Academic Encounters

2nd Edition

Jessica Williams
Series Editor: Bernard Seal

Studies 2

READING
WRITING

CAMBRIDGE
UNIVERSITY PRESS

CAMBRIDGE
UNIVERSITY PRESS

32 Avenue of the Americas, New York, NY 10013-2473, USA

Cambridge University Press is part of the University of Cambridge.

It furthers the University's mission by disseminating knowledge in the pursuit of education, learning and research at the highest international levels of excellence.

www.cambridge.org
Information on this title: www.cambridge.org/9781107627222

First published 1999
Second edition 2013
2nd printing 2014

Printed in the United States of America

A catalog record for this publication is available from the British Library.

ISBN 978-1-107-64791-6 Student's Book
ISBN 978-1-107-62722-2 Teacher's Manual

Additional resources for this publication at www.cambridge.org/academicencounters
Cambridge University Press has no responsibility for the persistence or accuracy of URLs for external or third-party Internet Web sites referred to in this publication and does not guarantee that any content on such Web sites is, or will remain, accurate or appropriate. Information regarding prices, travel timetables, and other factual information given in this work is correct at the time of first printing but Cambridge University Press does not guarantee the accuracy of such information thereafter.

Layout services: NETS, Bloomfield, CT

Table of Contents

Scope and Sequence

Unit 1: Laws of the Land • 1

	Content	**R** Reading Skills	**W** Writing Skills
Chapter 1 **The Foundations of Government** page 4	**Reading 1** From Colonies to United States **Reading 2** A Balance of Power **Reading 3** The Bill of Rights	Thinking about the topic Reading for main ideas Reading for details Personalizing the topic Examining graphics Predicting Applying what you have read Previewing art Reading critically Reading boxed texts	Showing contrast Writing definitions
Chapter 2 **Constitutional Issues Today** page 27	**Reading 1** Freedom of Expression: How Far Does it Go? **Reading 2** Separating Religion and Government **Reading 3** Guns in America: The Right to Bear Arms	Thinking about the topic Reading for main ideas Applying what you have read Examining graphics Reading for details Predicting Scanning	Writing about numbers Giving reasons Topic sentences

Unit 2: A Diverse Nation • 51

	Content	**R** Reading Skills	**W** Writing Skills
Chapter 3 **The Origins of Diversity** page 54	**Reading 1** America's First People **Reading 2** Slavery **Reading 3** A Country of Immigrants	Examining graphics Previewing art Reading for main ideas Reading for details Applying what you have read Thinking about the topic Reading boxed texts Predicting Scanning	The passive voice
Chapter 4 **Diversity in the United States Today** page 77	**Reading 1** America's Increasing Diversity **Reading 2** The Nation's Fastest-growing Minorities **Reading 3** The Undocumented: Unauthorized Immigrants	Increasing reading speed Examining graphics Thinking about the topic Reading for main ideas Reading actively Understanding cartoons	Writing descriptions Writing about growth

V Vocabulary Skills	**A** Academic Success Skills	Learning Outcomes
Guessing meaning from context Cues for finding word meaning Expressing permission	Making a vocabulary notebook Using a vocabulary notebook	Write a paragraph about an important right or freedom with a topic sentence and supporting details
Word families Collocations The Academic Word List	Taking notes with a chart Understanding test questions	

V Vocabulary Skills	**A** Academic Success Skills	Learning Outcomes
Words related to the topic Synonyms Guessing meaning from context	Highlighting Taking notes with a chart	Write two paragraphs about contrasting attitudes toward diversity
Suffixes Words related to the topic Using a dictionary	Answering true/false questions Taking notes in an outline	

Unit 3: The Struggle for Equality • 103

	Content	**R** Reading Skills	**W** Writing Skills
Chapter 5 **The Struggle Begins** page 106	**Reading 1** All Men Are Created Equal **Reading 2** The Legacy of the Civil War **Reading 3** The Civil Rights Movement and the Women's Movement	Increasing reading speed Thinking about the topic Predicting Reading for details Reading boxed texts Reading for main ideas Pronoun reference	Writing about time sequences
Chapter 6 **The Struggle Continues** page 127	**Reading 1** What Does Equality Mean Today? **Reading 2** Equal Rights and Protection for All **Reading 3** How Equal Are We Now?	Understanding key term Reading for main ideas Applying what you have read Predicting Thinking about the topic Reading for details Examining graphics Reading about statistics	Understanding text structure Markers of relationship Writing about examples Writing about obligations and recommendations Writing about statistics

Unit 4: American Values • 153

	Content	**R** Reading Skills	**W** Writing Skills
Chapter 7 **American Values from the Past** page 156	**Reading 1** The Roots of American Values **Reading 2** The American West **Reading 3** The Business of Success	Increasing reading speed Applying what you have read Previewing art Reading for details Examining graphics Thinking about the topic Predicting Understanding cartoons	Noun + infinitive phrases *Few* and *a few* Writing about change
Chapter 8 **American Values Today** page 180	**Reading 1** The Individual and Society: Rights and Responsibilities **Reading 2** The Open Road and Car Culture **Reading 3** Is the American Dream Still Possible?	Thinking about the topic Reading for main ideas Applying what you have read Previewing art Scanning Reading for details Examining graphics Reading actively	Understanding text structure Writing about reasons Gerunds Writing definitions

V Vocabulary Skills	A Academic Success Skills	Learning Outcomes
Suffixes Words related to the topic Guessing meaning from context Understanding key terms	Answering definition questions on a test Answering short-answer test questions	Write two paragraphs presenting a point of view on equal rights and equal protection
Synonyms Prepositions with verbs	Reviewing for a test	

V Vocabulary Skills	A Academic Success Skills	Learning Outcomes
Understanding key terms Word families Collocations	Preparing for a test Answering multiple-choice questions	Write a four-paragraph essay on American values
Prepositions Collocations Word families	Responding to a quote Answering true/false questions Conducting a survey	

Introduction

The *Academic Encounters* Series

Academic Encounters is a sustained content-based series for English language learners preparing to study college-level subject matter in English. The goal of the series is to expose students to the types of texts and tasks that they will encounter in their academic course work and provide them with the skills to be successful when that encounter occurs.

At each level in the series, there are two thematically paired books. One is an academic reading and writing skills book, in which students encounter readings that are based on authentic academic texts. In this book, students are given the skills to understand texts and respond to them in writing. The reading and writing book is paired with an academic listening and speaking skills book, in which students encounter discussion and lecture material specially prepared by experts in their field. In this book, students learn how to take notes from a lecture, participate in discussions, and prepare short presentations.

The books at each level may be used as stand-alone reading and writing books or listening and speaking books. Or they may be used together to create a complete four-skills course. This is made possible because the content of each book at each level is very closely related. Each unit and chapter, for example, has the same title and deals with similar content, so that teachers can easily focus on different skills, but the same content, as they toggle from one book to the other. Additionally, if the books are taught together, when students are presented with the culminating unit writing or speaking assignment, they will have a rich and varied supply of reading and lecture material to draw on.

A sustained content-based approach

The *Academic Encounters* series adopts a sustained content-based approach, which means that at each level in the series students study subject matter from one or two related academic content areas. There are two major advantages gained by students who study with materials that adopt this approach.

- Because all the subject matter in each book is related to a particular academic discipline, concepts and language tend to recur. This has a major facilitating effect. As students progress through the course, what at first seemed challenging feels more and more accessible. Students thus gain confidence and begin to feel that academic study in English is not as overwhelming a task as they might at first have thought.

- The second major advantage in studying in a sustained content-based approach is that students actually gain some in-depth knowledge of a particular subject area. In other content-based series, in which units go from one academic discipline to another, students' knowledge of any one subject area is inevitably superficial. However, after studying a level of *Academic Encounters* students may feel that they have sufficiently good grounding in the subject area that they may decide to move on to study the academic subject area in a mainstream class, perhaps fulfilling one of their general education requirements.

The four levels in the series

The *Academic Encounters* series consists of four pairs of books designed for four levels of student proficiency. Each pair of books focuses on one or more related academic subject areas commonly taught in college-level courses.

- *Academic Encounters* 1: The Natural World
  Level 1 in the series focuses on earth science and biology. The books are designed for students at the low-intermediate level.

- *Academic Encounters* 2: American Studies
  Level 2 in the series focuses on American history, politics, government, and culture. The books are designed for students at the intermediate level.
- *Academic Encounters* 3: Life in Society
  Level 3 in the series focuses on sociological topics. The books are designed for students at the high-intermediate level.
- *Academic Encounters* 4: Human Behavior
  Level 4 in the series focuses on psychology and human communication. The books are designed for students at the low-advanced to advanced level.

New in the Second Edition

The second edition of the *Academic Encounters* series retains the major hallmark of the series: the sustained content approach with closely related pairs of books at each level. However, lessons learned over the years in which *Academic Encounters* has been on the market have been heeded in the publication of this brand new edition. As a result, the second edition marks many notable improvements that will make the series even more attractive to the teacher who wants to fully prepare his or her students to undertake academic studies in English.

New in the series

Four units, eight chapters per level. The number of units and chapters in each level has been reduced from five units / ten chapters in the first edition to four units / eight chapters in the second edition. This reduction in source material will enable instructors to more easily cover the material in each book.

Increased scaffolding. While the amount of reading and listening material that students have to engage with has been reduced, there has been an increase in the number of tasks that help students access the source material, including a greater number of tasks that focus on the linguistic features of the source material.

Academic Vocabulary. In both the reading and writing and the listening and speaking books, there are tasks that now draw students' attention to the academic vocabulary that is embedded in the readings and lectures, including a focus on the Academic Word list (AWL). All the AWL words encountered during the readings and lectures are also listed in an appendix at the back of each book.

Full color new design. A number of features have been added to the design, not only to make the series more attractive, but more importantly to make the material easier to navigate. Each task is coded so that teachers and students can see at a glance what skill is being developed. In addition, the end-of-unit writing skill and speaking skill sections are set off in colored pages that make them easy to find.

New in the reading and writing books

More writing skill development. In the first edition of *Academic Encounters*, the reading and writing books focused primarily on reading skills. In the second edition, the two skills are much more evenly weighted, making these books truly reading and writing books.

End-of-chapter and unit writing assignments. At the end of each chapter and unit, students are taught about aspects of academic writing and given writing assignments. Step-by step scaffolding is provided in these sections to ensure that students draw on the content, skills, and language they studied in the unit; and can successfully complete the assignments.

New and updated readings. Because many of the readings in the series are drawn from actual discipline-specific academic textbooks, recent editions of those textbooks have been used to update and replace readings.

New in the listening and speaking books

More speaking skill development. In the first edition of *Academic Encounters*, the listening and speaking books focused primarily on listening skills. In the second edition, the two skills in each of the books are more evenly weighted.

End-of-unit assignments. Each unit concludes with a review of the academic vocabulary introduced in the unit, a topic review designed to elicit the new vocabulary, and an oral presentation related to the unit topics, which includes step-by-step guidelines in researching, preparing, and giving different types of oral presentations.

New and updated lectures and interviews. Because the material presented in the interviews and lectures often deals with current issues, some material has been updated or replaced to keep it interesting and relevant for today's students.

Video of the lectures. In addition to audio CDs that contain all the listening material in the listening and speaking books, the series now contains video material showing the lectures being delivered. These lectures are on DVD and are packaged in the back of the Student Books.

The *Academic Encounters* Reading and Writing Books

Skills

There are two main goals of the *Academic Encounters* reading and writing books. The first is to give students the skills and confidence to approach an academic text, read it efficiently and critically, and take notes that extract the main ideas and key details. The second is to enable students to display the knowledge that has been gained from the reading either in a writing assignment or in a test-taking situation.

To this end, tasks in the *Academic Encounters* reading and writing books are color-coded and labeled as R **(R)** *Reading Skill* tasks, V **(V)** *Vocabulary Skill* tasks, W **(W)** *Writing Skill* tasks, and A **(A)** *Academic Success* tasks. At the beginning of each unit, all the skills taught in the unit are listed in a chart for easy reference.

- **Reading Skills (R).** The reading skill tasks are designed to help students develop strategies before reading, while reading, and after reading. The pre-reading tasks, such as Skimming for Main Ideas, teach students strategies they can employ to facilitate their first reading of a text. Post-reading tasks, such as *Identifying Main Ideas* and *Reading Critically* give students the tools to gain the deepest understanding possible of the text.

- **Vocabulary Skills (V).** Vocabulary learning is an essential part of improving one's ability to read an academic text. Many tasks throughout the books focus on particular sets of vocabulary that are important for reading in a particular subject area as well as the sub-technical vocabulary that is important for reading in any academic discipline. At the end of each chapter, some of the AWL words that appeared in the readings of the chapter are listed and an exercise is given that checks students' knowledge of those words.

- **Writing Skills (W).** There are two types of writing skills throughout the books. One type might more accurately be described as reading-for-writing skills in that students are asked to notice features of the texts that they have been reading in order to gain insight into how writers construct text. The other type is writing development skills, and these appear in the mid-unit and end-of-unit writing sections and overtly instruct students how to write academic texts, in which main ideas are supported with examples and in which plagiarism is avoided.

- **Academic Success (A).** Besides learning how to read, write, and build their language proficiency, students also have to learn other skills that are particularly important in academic settings. These include such skills as learning how to prepare for a content test, answer certain types of test questions, take notes, and work in study groups. *Academic Encounters* makes sure that this important dimension of being a student in which English is the medium of instruction is not ignored.

Readings

There are three readings in each chapter of the *Academic Encounters* reading and writing books. Readings vary in length and difficulty depending on the level of the book. The readings in the upper two levels contain texts that in many cases are unchanged from the college textbooks from which they were taken. The readings in the two lower-level books make use of authentic source materials. They are adapted so that they can be better processed by lower-level students, but great pains have been taken to retain the authentic flavor of the original materials.

Tasks

Before and after each reading, students are given tasks that activate one or more of the target skills in the book. The first time a task is introduced in the book, it is accompanied by a colored commentary box that explains which skill is being practiced and why it is important. When the task type occurs again later in the book, it is sometimes accompanied by another commentary box, as a reminder or to present new information about the skill. At the back of the book, there is an alphabetized index of all the skills covered in the tasks.

Order of units

In each book, a rationale exists for the order of the unit topics. Teachers may choose a different order if they wish; however, because reading skills and writing skills are developed sequentially throughout the books, teaching the units in the order that they occur is optimal. If teachers do choose to teach the units out of order, they can refer to the Skills Index at the back of the book to see what types of tasks have been presented in earlier units and build information from those tasks into their lessons.

Course length

Each unit in the *Academic Encounters* reading and writing books will take approximately 20 hours to teach. The six readings per unit should take about two to two and a half hours to teach, with about twenty minutes to be spent on the pre-reading activities. The two academic writing development sections can be taught as two writing workshops, each taking roughly two to two and a half hours to teach.

The course can be made shorter or longer. To shorten the course, teachers might choose not to do every task in the book and to assign some tasks and texts as homework, rather than do them in class. To lengthen the course, teachers might choose to supplement the book with content-related material from their own files, to assign Internet research, and to spend more time on the writing assignments.

Unit Content Quizzes

The *Academic Encounters* series adopts a sustained content-based approach in which students experience what it is like to study an academic discipline in an English-medium instruction environment. In such classes, students are held accountable for learning the content of the course by the administering of tests.

In the *Academic Encounters* series, we also believe that students should go back and study the content of the book and prepare for a test. This review of the material in the books simulates the college learning experience, and makes students review the language and content that they have studied.

At the back of this *Teacher's Manual* are four reproducible content quizzes, one for each unit in the book. Each quiz contains a mixture of true/false questions, multiple choice, and short-answer questions, plus one question that requires a longer one- or two-paragraph answer. The tests should take about 50 minutes of class time. Students should be given time to prepare for the test, but should take it as soon as possible after completing the unit.

General Teaching Guidelines

In this section, we give some very general instructions for teaching the following elements that occur in each unit of the *Academic Encounters* listening and speaking books:

- The unit opener, which contains a preview of the unit content, skills, and learning outcomes
- The *Preparing to Read* sections, which occur before each reading
- The *Readings*, which are sometimes accompanied by short boxed readings
- The *After You Read* sections, which follow each reading
- The *Academic Vocabulary Review* sections, which are at the end of each chapter
- The *Developing Writing Skills* sections, which are at the end of the first chapter of each unit
- The *Practicing Academic Writing* sections, which occur at the end of the second chapter of each unit

Unit Opener

The opening page of the unit contains the title of the unit, a photograph that is suggestive of the content of the unit, and a brief paragraph that summarizes the unit. Make sure that students understand what the title means. Have them look at the art on the page and describe it and talk about how it might relate to the title.

Finally look at the summary paragraph at the bottom of the page. Read it with your students and check to be sure that they understand the vocabulary and key concepts. At this point it is not necessary to introduce the unit topics in any depth, since they will get a detailed preview of the contents of the unit on the third page of the unit.

On the second page of the unit, students can preview the chapter and reading titles and see what skills are being taught throughout the unit. Have students read and understand the chapter and reading titles, and then focus on a few of the skills listed. Note those that students might already be familiar with and some new ones that are being taught for the first time in the book. Draw students' attention to the *Learning Outcomes* at the bottom of the page. This alerts students to what they are expected to be able to do by the end of the unit. It is also essentially a preview of the major assignment of the unit.

On the third page of the unit are tasks that preview the unit either by having students predict what information they might find in each section of the unit or by giving them some information from the unit and having them respond to it. The first couple of times that you teach from this page, tell students that when they are given a longer reading assignment, such as a chapter of a textbook, it is always a good strategy for them to preview the titles and headings of the reading, predict what the reading might be about, and to think about what they might already know about the subject matter.

The unit opener section should take about an hour of class time.

Preparing to Read

Each reading is preceded by a page of pre-reading tasks in a section called Preparing to Read. Pre-reading is heavily emphasized in the *Academic Encounters* reading and writing books since it is regarded as a crucial step in the reading process. Some pre-reading activities introduce students to new vocabulary; some teach students to get an overall idea of the content by surveying the text for headings, graphic material, captions, and art, and others have students recall their prior knowledge of the topic and their personal experiences to help them assimilate the material that they are about to encounter in the reading.

Although one or two pre-reading tasks are always included for each text, you should look for ways to supplement these tasks with additional pre-reading activities. As you and your students work your way through the book, students will become exposed to more and more pre-reading strategies. Having been exposed to these, students should be adding them to their repertoire, and you should encourage their regular use. For example, after having practiced the skill of examining graphic material, previewing headings and subheadings, and skimming for main ideas, students should ideally carry out these operations every time they approach a new reading.

As a general principle, the lower the proficiency level of the students, the greater is the need to spend time on the pre-reading activities. The more pre-reading tasks students undertake, the easier it is for students to access the text when it comes time for them to do a close reading.

Each *Preparing to Read* page should take about thirty minutes of class time. Some may require more or less time.

Reading

Once it comes time for students to read the text, how closely should they do so at this point? Some students believe that after doing the *Preparing to Read* tasks, they should now read the text slowly and carefully. They will be particularly tempted to do so because the texts have been crafted to be intentionally challenging for them, since students need to be prepared to read challenging, authentic, un-simplified text in their academic studies. However, students should be discouraged from doing this. For one thing, it is a poor use of class time to have students poring silently over a text for 20 minutes or more. More importantly, it is vital that students train themselves to read quickly, tolerating some ambiguity and going for understanding the main ideas and overall text structure, rather than every word and detail.

To promote faster reading, the book includes one *Increasing Reading Speed* task in most of the units. In this task, students are encouraged to read the text as quickly as possible, using techniques that can help them read faster while retaining a fairly high level of comprehension. If students consistently apply these techniques, most texts will take between 3 and 7 minutes to read. Before students start reading any text, therefore, it is a good idea to give them a challenging time limit, which they should aim toward to complete their reading of the text.

An alternative to reading every text in class is to assign some of the longer texts as homework. When you do this, you should do the pre-reading tasks in class at the end of the lesson and start the next class by having students quickly skim the text again before moving on to the *After You Read* tasks.

After You Read

Sometimes, after students have completed reading the text, the first order of business is not to move on to the *After You Read* tasks, but to revisit the Preparing to Read tasks to check to see if students had the correct answers in a predicting or skimming activity.

The tasks in the *After You Read* section are varied. Some focus on the content of the reading, some on the linguistic features of the reading, such as the vocabulary and grammar, and some on the organization of the text. There are also tasks that teach study skills. No two *After You Read* sections are the same (in fact, no two *After You Read* tasks are quite the same) because the content, organization, and the language of the reading dictate the types of tasks that would be appropriate.

Teachers who are used to more conventional post-reading tasks may be surprised to find that the focus of the post-reading is not text comprehension. This is because the intention of every task in the *Academic Encounters* reading and writing books is to develop a skill, not to test comprehension.

The following are the main functions of the post-reading activities in the *Academic Encounters* reading and writing books:

- to have students read for main ideas and think critically about the text
- to ask students to think about the content of the text, find a personal connection to it, or apply new information learned from the text in some way
- to highlight some of the most salient language in the text, either vocabulary or grammatical structures, and have students use that language in some way
- to have students gain insight into the style and organization of the text and to use those insights to help them become more effective writers themselves
- to develop students' repertoire of study skills by teaching them, for example, how to highlight a text, take notes, and summarize
- to develop students' test-preparation skills by familiarizing them with certain question types and by asking them to assess what they would need to do if they were going to be tested on the text.

To make the course as lively as possible, student interaction has been built into most activities. Thus, although the books are primarily intended to build reading and writing skills, opportunities for speaking abound. Students discuss the content of the texts, they work collaboratively to solve task problems, they compare answers in pairs or small groups, and sometimes they engage in role-playing.

Academic Vocabulary Review

The final exercise of each chapter lists words from the Academic Word List that students encountered in the chapter readings. The first time that you do this exercise, discuss the meaning of "academic word." Tell students that it is a word that occurs frequently across all types of academic texts regardless of the academic subject matter. As such, these are words that deserve students' special attention. Encourage students to learn these words and point out that at the back of the book there is an appendix of words from the Academic Word List that occurred in the readings. Promote the value of learning words from this appendix during their study of the course.

Developing Writing Skills

The *Developing Writing Skills* section of the unit occurs in the middle of the unit between the two chapters. In this section, students learn about some aspect of the writing process, such as how to write topic sentences, how to organize a paragraph or an essay, how to summarize, and how to avoid plagiarism. In the *Academic Encounters* reading and writing books Levels 1-2, the focus is primarily on learning how to write paragraphs. In the higher two levels, 3-4, the focus is on longer pieces of text, including academic essays.

In the first part of the section, the particular sub-skill that is the focus of the section is presented in an information box with clear examples. In the second part of the section, students are given a number of discrete activities to practice these writing sub-skills. Many of the activities in this section are collaborative. Teachers might therefore want to set up a writing workshop-style classroom when working on these sections, putting the students to work in pairs or small groups and circulating among them, checking on their progress and giving individualized feedback.

Practicing Academic Writing

The two sections of the unit that are devoted entirely to writing instruction are both set off on lightly-colored pages so that teachers can easily locate them throughout the book. This enables teachers or students to use them as reference sections and come back to them frequently as they work their way through the book.

The second writing section, *Practicing Academic Writing*, occurs at the very end of the unit. In this section, students are given a writing assignment and guided through steps in the writing process to help them satisfactorily complete the assignment. The writing assignments draw from content from the unit, so students are asked to go back to the readings in order to complete the assignments. In addition, students are reminded of any linguistic features that were the focus of instruction in the unit and are prompted to attempt to use such language in their own writing.

The *Practicing Academic Writing* section is divided into three parts: Preparing to Write, Now Write, and After You Write. In these three parts, students do pre-writing work (Preparing to Write), write a first draft (Now Write), and revise and edit their work (After You Write).

The *Practicing Academic Writing* section may well stretch over two or more class periods, with teachers varying the amount of in-class and out-of-class time spent on writing. The Preparing to Write part should be done in class. Here the students are presented with the assignment and are given some pre-writing activities that will aid them in writing their first draft. The *Now Write* part should at least sometimes be done in class so that teachers can accurately assess the strength of a student's writing.

It is recommended that teachers go through the *After You Write* part of the section in a different class from the first two parts of this section, so that they have a chance to provide feedback on students' writing and students have a chance to digest and apply that feedback. Remind students that good writers almost always write and re-write their texts several times and that the more re-writing of their texts that they do, the better writers they will eventually become.

Chapter 1
The Foundations of Government

Reading 1 – From Colonies to United States

After You Read

1 Reading for main ideas Page 7
A

1. 2   2. 3   3. 3   4. 2   5. 4
6. 1   7. 1   8. 4

B

1. b   2. b   3. a   4. a

2 Reading for details Page 8
1. 4   2. 1   3. 2   4. 3   5. 1
6. 4   7. 2   8. 4

3 Guessing meaning from context Page 8
B
Clues:
1. that is   2. that is   3. in other words

C
Sample answers:
1. A republic is a government with an elected leader instead of a king.
2. A democratic government is a system based on the idea that all men are equal and that the government should represent all of the nation's citizens.
3. A federalist system is a system that divides power and responsibility between the states and the federal, or central, government.

Reading 2 – A Balance of Power

Preparing to Read

1 Examining graphics Page 10
A

1. C   2. C   3. P   4. SC   5. C
6. P   7. C   8. P

After You Read

1 Cues for finding word meaning Page 13
A

- reject (Par. 3)
- not permitted by the Constitution (Par. 3)
- a balance of power between the federal, or central, government and the state governments (Par. 5)

B
1. the highest court   2. block   3. Congress

C
1. Congress   2. blocks   3. reject

D
1. the highest court   2. central
3. not permitted by the Constitution

E
Sample answers:
The judicial branch is the Supreme Court and other courts. Electing, or choosing, a national leader is very important.

2 Examining graphics Page 14
B

1. F   2. T   3. T   4. T   5. F
6. F   7. T   8. F

3 Showing contrast Page 15
A

- They wanted a strong leader; <u>however</u>, they also wanted a representative government. (Par. 1)
- <u>Although</u> people often think of the president as the center of government, the Constitution lists the legislative branch first. (Par. 2)
- <u>However</u>, if two-thirds of the members in both the Senate and the House of Representatives disagree, they can override, that is, reject, the president's veto. (Par. 3)
- <u>Although</u> the Constitution does not establish political parties, there have been two strong parties in the United States throughout most of its history. (Par. 4)

B

Sample answers:

Although the president leads the military, only Congress can declare war.

Although the president leads the military, he cannot declare war.

The president leads the military. However, only Congress can declare war.

Reading 3 The Bill of Rights

Preparing to Read

1 Thinking about the topic Page 16
A

The following activities are legal in the United States: 2, 6, 8. All others are unconstitutional.

After You Read

1 Applying what you have read Page 20
B

1. a   2. b   3. c   4. a   5. a
6. a   7. b   8. a   9. c

C

1. b   2. a   3. a   4. a   5. a
6. b   7. c   8. a

3 Expressing permission Pages 21–22
A

- . . . [T]he First Amendment <u>does allow</u> people to protest against the government if they think it is doing something wrong. (Par. 4)
- It <u>permits</u> them to criticize the government in speech or in writing. (Par. 4)
- The Second Amendment <u>permits</u> states to form a militia, or army of citizens, and citizens to keep guns for their own protection. (Par. 5)
- The Fourth Amendment <u>forbids</u> police searches without permission from a judge. (Par. 5)
- Before the Nineteenth Amendment (1920), women were <u>prohibited</u> from voting in most states. (Boxed text, top p. 19)

B

1. may   2. may not   3. may   4. may not

C

Sample answers:

2. The Bill of Rights permits criticism of the government.
3. The Bill of Rights does allow freedom of speech.
4. The Bill of Rights prohibits police searches without permission from a judge.
5. The Bill of Rights allows gun ownership.
6. The Bill of Rights forbids imprisonment without an explanation.
7. The Bill of Rights does not permit secret trials.

E

Sample answers:

2. The Bill of Rights forbids <u>the police</u> to <u>search without permission from a judge</u>.
3. The Bill of Rights permits <u>citizens</u> to <u>criticize the government</u>.
4. The Bill of Rights allows <u>citizens</u> to <u>express their ideas freely</u>.

4 Writing definitions Page 22
B

Sample answers:

1. A criminal suspect is <u>a person</u> who <u>is accused of a crime</u>.
2. Libel is <u>a lie</u> that <u>could harm someone</u>.
3. The Bill of Rights is a <u>document</u> that <u>establishes many fundamental rights and freedoms</u>.
4. Suffragettes were <u>women</u> who <u>fought for their right to vote</u>.

Chapter 1 Academic Vocabulary Review

Page 24

1. framework
2. maintain
3. consists
4. rejected
5. removed
6. documents
7. fundamental
8. assistance
9. guarantees
10. specifies

Developing Writing Skills

Pages 25–26

A

1. One of the main purposes of the Bill of Rights was to limit the power of government, but this idea is also clear in some more recent amendments.
2. One of the most important and powerful is the Fourteenth Amendment.
3. However, repealing, that is, reversing, an amendment is even more uncommon.

B

1. this idea is also clear in some more recent amendments
2. One of the most important and powerful
3. is even more uncommon

C

2, 5, 6

D

Sample answers:

a. The Constitution is the most important document in U.S. history.
b. The first settlers in the United States hoped to start a new life.
c. Freedom of expression is a complicated idea.
d. Criminal suspects have important rights.
e. Voting rights have a long history of struggle.
f. *Answers will vary.*

Chapter 2
Constitutional Issues Today

Reading 1 – Freedom of Expression: How Far Does It Go?

After You Read

1 Reading for main ideas Page 31
A

1. 3   2. 6   3. 2   4. 4   5. 5/6

B
2.

2 Taking notes with a chart Pages 31–32
A

Sample answers:

	Protected	Not Protected
Hate speech and symbols	1. *saying offensive or hurtful things about people* 2. *burning crosses to express ideas*	1. *saying or writing offensive things about people in a way that threatens them* 2. *burning crosses to encourage violence*
Political protest	1. *protest marches or demonstrations* 2. *flag burning*	1. *protests that block public streets* 2. *protests that prevent offices or business from operating*

B

Sample answers:

- The First Amendment does not protect hate speech that contains threats.
- There is no protection for political protests that prevent others from doing what they want to do, such as go to work or school.

3 Word families Pages 32–33
A

1. global
2. religious
3. race
4. hurtful
5. controversy
6. political

B

1. harmful
2. dangerous
3. presidential
4. central
5. painful
6. courageous

4 Collocations Page 33
A

(agree) with; (participated) in; (protesting) against

B

Sample answers:

It is legal to write about government programs that you do not agree with.

Many people participated in the Occupy movement.

The right to protest against the government is protected by the First Amendment.

Reading 2 – Separating Religion and Government

After You Read

1 Reading for details Pages 37
A

(sent. 2) It states that the government may not interfere with people's private religious beliefs.

B

Sample answers (all from paragraph 2):

- The government may not establish a church or force people to practice a particular religion.
- It may not favor or support one religion more than another.
- [T]his means that religious practices and symbols are not permitted on government property, such as courts or public (government-supported) schools.
- [T]eachers in public schools may not say prayers in class.
- This guarantee of religious freedom also means that individuals may not impose their religious beliefs on others.

2 Writing about numbers Page 37
B

Sample answers:

- Just over three-quarters of Americans are Christians.
- About four percent of Americans do not have a religion.
- Approximately one percent of Americans are Buddhists.

3 The Academic Word List Page 38

1. i   2. d   3. a   4. g   5. b
6. j   7. e   8. c   9. h   10. f

5 Giving reasons Page 39
A

1. The authors of the Constitution included religious freedom in the First Amendment because they wanted to avoid religious conflicts.
2. The Constitution establishes a policy of "separation of church and state"; therefore, there is no national religion.
3. Because the early settlers were Christian, some Americans think of their country as a Christian nation.
4. Since the Supreme Court has ruled that flag burning is a legal form of political protest, any law that prohibits it is unconstitutional.

B

Sample answers:

1. Since the government cannot support a religion, religious practices and symbols are not permitted on government property, such as courts and public schools.
2. Many people left Europe for the American colonies because they wanted a chance for success.
3. The Fourth Amendment prohibits unreasonable searches; therefore, the police cannot enter a house without permission from a judge.
4. The police said protestors were harming the health and safety of other people; as a result, they ended the Occupy protests.

Reading 3 – Guns in America: The Right to Bear Arms

After You Read

1 Scanning Page 43

1. Wild animals, British army (Par. 2)
2. an army of citizens (Par. 3)

3. broad (Par. 9)
4. 300 million (Par. 9)
5. 12 (Par. 10)

2 Topic sentences Page 43
A and B

3. A   5. F

4 Understanding test questions Page 45
A

a. Type 2   d. Type 2
b. Type 3   e. Type 2
c. Type 1   f. Type 3

B

a. Type 2   b. Type 3   c. Type 1

Chapter 2 Academic Vocabulary Review Page 46

1. majority   6. controversial
2. Immigrants   7. contribute
3. widespread   8. restrictions
4. residents   9. individuals
5. participate   10. security

Practicing Academic Writing

Preparing to Write Page 48
C and D

3 I am afraid of the police. Without this protection, they could come into my house.
3 A newspaper story said the police put drugs into someone's car during a search and then arrested the owner. That is breaking the law.
1 Criminals might be hiding things like drugs and guns in their house or car.
3 What if a police officer is just mad at you and wants to do something bad to you?
2 It is hard for the police to find criminals if there are too many laws that protect the criminals.
2 Maybe the police are trying too hard to find criminals and they break the law, too.

Chapter 3
The Origins of Diversity

Reading 1 – America's First People

Preparing to Read

1 Examining graphics Page 54

Sample answer:
The loss of Native American land

2 Previewing art Page 54

Sample answers:
1. They gave up their culture.
2. They show the dramatic losses of Native Americans.

After You Read

1 Reading for main ideas Page 58
2

2 Reading for details Page 58
C and D

Key term/ point 1: government policies	Key term/ point 2: attitudes of white Americans	Key term/ point 3: damaged/ destroyed native communities
government broke treaties	settlers believed in ownership of land	Europeans brought diseases that killed many natives
government passed laws that forced native tribes off their lands to reservations	white Americans believed they were better than Indians	settlers wanted Indians' rich land; battles with government began, Indians usually the loser
government's assimilation policy made native children learn American culture		children taken from their families and put in boarding schools

3 The passive voice Page 59
A

1. Many native communities <u>were</u> almost <u>destroyed</u> by the actions of the settlers and the policies of the American government.
2. Sometimes a tribe <u>was allowed</u> to stay on a small part of its original land.
3. Hundreds of Cherokee <u>were beaten, imprisoned,</u> or <u>murdered</u>.
4. The Cherokee who survived <u>were forced</u> to march 1,000 miles.

B

<u>Many native children were required</u> to leave their families and attend government boarding schools. The children lived at these schools, where their <u>traditional ways were replaced</u> by the customs and behavior of white Americans.

C

1. is called
2. were imprisoned or killed
3. broke
4. were forced
5. created

D

Sample answer:
Native Americans were treated very badly by the U.S. government.

Reading 2 – Slavery

Preparing to Read

1 Words related to the topic Page 60
B

2. Sample answers:
furniture, equipment, land, animals, property

After You Read

1 Highlighting Page 64
A

Sample answers:

Unlike most of the people who have come to America, these Africans were brought against their will. Many of them died either in Africa before the journey or during the journey across the Atlantic Ocean, which lasted about seven weeks. The conditions on ships were dreadful; the passengers were often chained side by side, with no space to move. Experts estimate that between 10 and 25 percent of the slaves died on the journey. The ones who survived were sold. Husbands and wives, children and parents were often separated. They became the property of the people who bought them, with no rights of their own. They had to work long hours; most worked in the cotton fields, up to 16 hours a day during the harvest. They received poor food, and rough clothing and housing. If they disobeyed orders or tried to escape, the punishment was severe and painful. Women had to work until childbirth and return to work immediately afterward. Children began working at the age of five, and many died when they were very young. Some slaves, especially those who worked inside their owners' houses, lived in better conditions. These "house slaves" still had hard lives, however, and they had no freedom. The average life of a slave was very short – just 22 years – half that of whites at that time.

C

Sample answers:

The slaves received their freedom at the end of the American Civil War (1861–1865) which divided the North and the South. Disagreement about slavery was one of the major causes of the war. The South wanted to preserve slavery; it was essential to their prosperity. The North wanted to end it. (Par. 5)

2 Examining graphics Page 65
A

	Where picked up?	Where shipped to?
slaves	Africa	Ports in the Caribbean and American South
molasses	Caribbean	Northern U.S. cities
rum	Northern U.S. cities	Africa
cotton	Southern U.S.	Northern U.S. and Great Britain

B

1. The chart shows a list of various types of goods and people who were transported to and from different places.
2. The map shows how the triangular trade of slaves, molasses, and rum was connected to the cotton industry.
3. Student responses will vary.

3 Synonyms Page 66
A

1. essential
2. labor
3. opposed
4. profited
5. producers
6. dreadful
7. disobeyed
8. preserve
9. prosperity
10. narratives

5 The passive voice Page 67
A and B

Sample answers:

In the Caribbean ports, the ships picked up molasses, a syrup from Caribbean sugar, and brought it to northern cities such as Boston and New York. The molasses was then made into rum, an alcoholic drink. Some of the rum was shipped to Africa and traded for slaves. The slaves were then shipped to the Caribbean, and the cycle began again.

C

Sample answers with key word bolded:

1. In factories in England, the cotton was woven into **cloth**. The cloth was sold all over the world.
2. The sugar was cooked and made into **molasses**. The molasses was exchanged for African slaves.
3. The ships that returned to the ports in the Caribbean were filled with **slaves**. The slaves were sold at auctions.

Reading 3 – A Country of Immigrants

After You Read

1 Taking notes with a chart Page 72
B

Sample chart:

Pushes	Pulls	Barriers
religious persecution in Europe wars and revolutions poor economic conditions	adventure cheap land economic opportunity government encouragement	quotas and restrictions on immigration

2 Guessing meaning from context Page 73
B

1. N

However, this <u>flood</u> of immigrants began to **alarm** many American citizens. They believed that the immigrants, who worked for low wages, were <u>taking their jobs</u>.

2. N

Most immigrants had <u>difficult lives</u> but two immigrant groups who faced particular **hardships** in the second half of the nineteenth century were the Chinese and the Irish.

3. N

As they had with the Chinese, many Americans believed the Irish were <u>taking away their jobs</u> and as a result, the Irish, too, often faced **hostility**.

4. P

Quotas were <u>only for white immigrants; nonwhite immigrants were prohibited from entering the country at that time</u>. This quota system, which **favored** immigrants from Europe, ended in 1965.

3 Examining graphics Page 73
A

1. 1901–1910   2. No

B

question 1:

From 1820 to 1875, about 7 million newcomers entered the United States, but the greatest numbers came between 1875 and 1920. During this period, about 24 million immigrants poured into the United States from almost every part of the world, <u>reaching a peak in the first 10 years of the twentieth century</u>. (Par. 2)

question 2:

In response to fears about the flood of newcomers, <u>Congress passed a law to limit immigration</u>. It allowed only immigrants who could read and write. It also prohibited all immigration from Asia. In 1921, Congress established a system of quotas. (Par. 5)

4 Scanning Page 73

1. 24 million (Par. 2)
2. mining, building the railroad (Par. 3)
3. 1921 (Par. 5)
4. 1965 (Par. 5)
5. Cuba (Boxed text)

Chapter 3 Academic Vocabulary Review

Page 74

1. identity
2. survived
3. cycles
4. policy
5. primarily
6. construction
7. resources
8. cooperation
9. estimate
10. challenge

Developing Writing Skills

Pages 75–76

D

Sample answers:

	Native Americans	Enslaved Africans	Immigrants
Government laws and policies	*Removal Act*	*state permitted slavery and mistreatment*	*quotas and restrictions*
Working conditions		*long hours, poor conditions, severe punishment*	*dangerous difficult work, low wages*
Physical violence and mistreatment	*forced marches from land, children taken from families*	*physical mistreatment, families separated*	*violence against new immigrants*
Cultural differences	*no understanding of their culture*	*no understanding of their culture; whites believed they had none*	*misunderstanding of cultures that were different from American culture*
Attitudes of other groups	*government and white Americans viewed them as children*	*many viewed them as property like animals*	*many other groups were hostile*
Other			

G

Sample answers:

1. Physical violence and mistreatment were common problems for immigrants, slaves, and Native Americans.
   a. Immigrants were often beaten by Americans or members of earlier immigrant groups.
   b. Slaves were often terribly mistreated. They were whipped and beaten if they disobeyed their owners.
   c. Native Americans were forced on long marches.

H

Sample answers:

2. One of the hardest challenges for some groups was the destruction of their families and culture.
   a. Native Americans were forced to leave their traditional lands. Their children were taken away to attend boarding schools where they lost their culture.
   b. African families were destroyed when husbands, wives, and children were sold to different owners.
   c. Immigrants' cultures were often misunderstood.

Chapter 4
Diversity in Today's United States

Reading 1 – America's Increasing Diversity

Preparing to Read

1 Increasing reading speed Page 77
C

1. Since 1965, there has been a sharp increase in immigration from Latin America and Asia. Prior to that, European immigrants were the majority.
2. The white population (non-Latino) is about 63 percent.
3. Critics claim immigrants take jobs away from Americans, keep wages low, use too many public resources, and do not want to learn English or become part of American culture.

2 Examining graphics Page 77
A

Sample answer:

The chart shows that the majority of immigrants now come from Latin America and Asia.

After You Read

1 Answering true/false questions Page 81
A and B

1. T/Text
2. F/Text
3. F/Text
4. F/Text, Fig. 4.1
5. F/Text
6. F/Boxed Text

2 Writing descriptions Page 82
A

Sample answers:

2. living in the United States were born in another country
   who live in the United States were born in another country
3. criticizing new immigrants
   that criticized new immigrants
4. working in high-tech companies are immigrants
   who work in high-tech companies are immigrants

B

Sample answers:
1. Students taking important exams should sleep at least eight hours the night before the exams.
2. People learning a second language should find native speakers to practice with.
3. Tourists visiting Mexico should go to the National Museum in Mexico City.
4. People earning more than 1 million dollars a year should give some of their money to people in need.

3 Suffixes Pages 82–83
A

diversity (Par. 2), majority (Par. 5), minority (Par. 4), popularity (Par. 5), productivity (Par. 8)

B

1. diversity
2. equal
3. majority
4. legal
5. reality

C

Sample answers:

1. There has often been hostility against immigrants who look different.
2. Employers cannot treat workers differently because of their ethnicity.

Reading 2 – The Nation's Fastest-Growing Minorities

Preparing to Read

Examining graphics Page 84
B

Sample answers:
1. Midwest (North Dakota) and West (Nevada); also Southeast, Southwest
2. the East and Midwest/Southeast and West (Nevada and Utah); also Northwest
3. No, it is the percentage change, not the size of the population; that is, it indicates by what percent the population has increased or decreased.

After You Read

1 Reading for main ideas Page 88

A

a. 3   b. 4   c. 2   d. 1   e. 5

B

d c a b e

2 Taking notes in an outline Page 88

Sample answers:

The nation's fastest-growing minorities
I. The Asian American and Latino populations are growing faster than the white and black populations.
A. Latinos a larger minority than African Americans
B. more than 100,000,000 Latinos in 2050
C. Asian Americans are growing fastest
D. In 2050 – more than 35,000,000 Asian Americans in the nation
II. Latinos are the largest minority in the nation.
A. growing four times faster than the rest of the population
B. Latinos 50 percent of the growth in the U.S. population 2000–2010
III. Latinos no longer live only in big cities.
A. smaller cities and towns
B. in the country where there are not big towns at all
IV. Asian immigrants today are very different from the Asian immigrants of the past.
A. left their countries because there were no opportunities there
B. today many countries in Asia have many economic opportunities
V. Asians continue to immigrate to the U.S. for job opportunities.
A. they work in jobs that require a lot of education and skill
B. high incomes

3 Examining graphics Page 89

A

1. F   2. M   3. F   4. F
5. F   6. F   7. M

B

Sample answers:

1. The rapid increase in the Latino population could mean that political parties will try to target Latinos with their candidates and be more responsive to issues facing Latino immigrants.
2. The increase in the Asian American population could also mean that political parties will try to be more responsive to issues of Asian Americans, but probably not to the same extent as for the Latino population, given the smaller increases.
3. In both cases of rising populations, it could point to a more diverse group of politicians in the future, as the white population becomes a smaller percentage of the whole.
4. The increase in the Latino population is much faster and greater than that of the Asian American population, and therefore there is likely to be more attention given to Latinos in this regard.

4 Writing about growth Page 90

A

significant and continuous growth (Par. 1)
grew faster (Par. 1)
expand by 43 percent (Par. 2)
growing rapidly (Par. 4)

B

Sample answers:

1. The Latino population has increased faster than the Asian American population.
2. There has been steady growth in the Latino population in the last 10 years.
3. The Asian American population is expanding rapidly.

Reading 3 – The Undocumented: Unauthorized Immigrants

Preparing to Read

1 Words related to the topic Page 91
B

Sample answers:
- Most of the undocumented residents in the U.S. come from Mexico.
- More than 10 percent of the unauthorized immigrants in the nation were born in Asia.

After You Read

1 Reading actively Page 95
B

Most unauthorized immigrants enter the United States through the desert across the U.S.-Mexico border. These numbers have declined in recent years <u>for several reasons</u>. <u>First</u>, the economy of Mexico has improved since 2000, when about 500,000 people crossed the border illegally every year in search of work. <u>In addition</u>, the U.S. economy has been weak, so there are fewer jobs. <u>As a result</u>, the number of Mexicans crossing the border illegally is now estimated to be about 150,000 per year. Experts believe more people are returning to Mexico from the United States than are coming from Mexico to the United States.

D

Crossing the border can be dangerous. The United States watches many of the crossing points and stops any unauthorized immigrants who try to cross. <u>As a result</u>, many people have tried to cross from Mexico to the United States through the desert, at points where there are few U.S. officials. <u>Some</u> of them do not bring enough food or water. <u>Some</u> get lost. <u>Other</u> people hide in ships and trucks. In 2010, U.S. officials stopped about half a million people from illegally entering the country. They <u>also</u> found the bodies of more than 400 people who died on the journey.

2 Using a dictionary Page 96
B

1 support   1 treat   2 support

4 Understanding cartoons Page 97
B

Sample answers:

1 unauthorized immigrants
2 Native Americans
3 opponents of illegal immigration

Chapter 4 Academic Vocabulary Review

Page 98

1. predict
2. founders
3. income
4. dominant
5. approximately
6. debated
7. stable
8. targets
9. minimum
10. declined

Practicing Academic Writing

Preparing to Write

Page 100

F

a, c

Sample answers:

All of the paragraphs begin with a discussion of discrimination against Chinese in the workplace in the nineteenth century. Paragraph #2 continues with the topic of discrimination against Chinese in the nineteenth century, extending it beyond the workplace to other aspects of their lives. Paragraph #3 continues with the topic of workplace discrimination against Chinese, extending it into the present. Both establish unity by extending one aspect of the topic introduced in the beginning of the paragraph. Paragraph #1 introduced a new topic: discrimination outside of the workplace in this century. As a result, the paragraph is not unified.

Now Write

Pages 101–102

A

Sample answers:

Americans have often had a very positive perspective on immigration.
Americans have sometimes treated new immigrants badly.

B

Americans have often had a very positive perspective on immigration. Most Americans have immigrant origins and they are very proud of this fact. They also value the role that immigrants play in the economy. They want immigrants to do the work they do not want to do, such as gardening and cleaning.

Americans have sometimes treated new immigrants badly. This is especially true when the new immigrants come from a very different culture and Americans find their values and customs difficult to understand. Competition for jobs between Americans and new immigrants can also result in hostility.

C

Throughout history Americans have had an ambivalent attitude toward immigrants and immigration.

D

On the other hand, Americans have sometimes treated new immigrants badly.

Chapter 5
The Struggle Begins

Reading 1 – All Men Are Created Equal

Preparing to Read

1 Increasing reading speed Page 106
D

Sample answers:

1. the meaning of equality to the founders of the United States
2. all men are created equal
3. blacks and women had to be included as equal
4. to guarantee equal protection to everyone in the United States

After You Read

2 Writing about time sequences Pages 109–110
A

Sample answers:

- But what did the term *equality* really mean <u>when</u> the nation began? (Par. 1)
- <u>When</u> the Declaration of Independence and the Constitution were written, "men" did not mean "people." (Par. 4)
- Almost 100 years <u>after</u> the Declaration of Independence, the United States fought a **civil war** that involved the issue of equality. (Par. 5)
- <u>During</u> the Civil War, at a service to dedicate a cemetery for soldiers, President Abraham Lincoln made one of the most famous speeches in American history, the Gettysburg Address. (Par. 6)
- The Fourteenth Amendment to the Constitution was passed several years <u>after</u> the Civil War ended. (Par. 7)
- Yet, long <u>after</u> the Civil War, many Americans still did not receive equal treatment at work, at school, or in the courts. (Par. 7)

B

1. (After the Civil War / After the Civil War ended,) Congress passed the Thirteenth, Fourteenth, and Fifteenth Amendments.
2. (During) the second half of the twentieth century, there was an increase in immigration from Latin America.
3. (Before the War of Independence / Before the War of Independence began,) many colonists were British subjects.

3 Suffixes Page 110

1. exclusion
2. treatment
3. rejected
4. dedication
5. acceptance

Nouns [verb forms in text]	Verbs [noun forms in text]
accept	disagreement
include	protection
exclude	treatment
involve	
reject	
dedicate	

Reading 2 – The Legacy of the Civil War

Preparing to Read

1 Words related to the topic Page 111
B

Sample answers:

1. discrimination, segregation
2. segregation is forced separation and the practice of keeping ethnic, racial, religious, or gender groups separate

After You Read

1 Reading for details Page 114
A

Sample answers:

1. African Americans who tried to work against this system, even in small ways – for example, by arguing with a white person – <u>might be beaten, or worse, *lynched*. A lynching is a murder that occurs, usually by hanging,</u> when an angry individual or group decides that someone is guilty of a crime or misbehavior and kills the suspect without a trial. <u>It is estimated that there were almost 5,000 lynchings between 1882 and 1968.</u> (Par. 6)

2. Starting in the 1880s, most Southern states passed laws requiring African Americans to <u>pass *literacy tests* or pay a *voting tax* in order to vote.</u> Literacy tests required voters to read a text and answer questions about it. Often these texts were difficult and confusing. <u>Because most African Americans had little or no education at that time, many of them failed the test.</u> The voting tax required voters to pay to vote. <u>The voting tax was one or two dollars, which was equal to several days' wages</u> and far too expensive for many of the former slaves. The test and the tax were effective ways to prevent African Americans from voting. (Par. 2)

   <u>In addition, many Southern states passed grandfather laws, which stated that anyone with a family member (such as a grandfather) who had voted before 1867 did not have to take the literacy test or pay voting taxes.</u> This allowed uneducated, poor white voters to avoid these tests and taxes. Because the parents and grandparents of African Americans had been slaves and therefore unable to vote, the grandfather laws prevented many African Americans in the South from voting. (Par. 3)
3. <u>The white facilities were almost always superior to the facilities for African Americans.</u> (Par. 4)
4. In spite of the hardships, the period between the Civil War and the 1960s was a time of great cultural and artistic activity in the African American community. <u>There was also an increase in the number of businesses operated by and for African Americans. Madam C. J. Walker ran one of the most successful businesses during this time.</u> (Boxed text)
5. <u>The struggle for equality was not over.</u> From the beginning of the nation, through the Civil War, and still today, Americans have argued about what equality really means, and <u>the fight for equality for all people has been long and difficult.</u> (Par. 7)

2 Answering definition questions on a test Page 114

B

Sample answers:

1. **Literacy tests** were tests that required people to read something and answer questions about it before they could vote.
2. A **voting tax** was a fee that people had to pay in order to vote.
3. A **lynching** is a murder, usually by hanging, that is committed by angry people who kill because of the person's race or ethnicity.

C

Sample answer:

Jim Crow laws are laws that encourage segregation and discrimination. For example, some Jim Crow laws required separate public facilities for whites and blacks.

3 Reading boxed texts Page 115

B

Give some information or ideas that may be in conflict with the text.

4 Guessing meaning from context Pages 115–116

A

1. b   2. a   3. c   4. a

B

Sample answer:

between races

Reading 3 – The Battle for Civil Rights

After You Read

1 Reading for main ideas Page 121

4

2 Pronoun reference Page 121

1. In 1957, the Arkansas governor tried to prevent <u>African American students</u> from attending the all-white high school in the state capital, Little Rock. President Dwight Eisenhower had to send in soldiers to protect **them**.
2. <u>Some communities</u> closed **their** public schools because **they** did not want black children to attend. <u>Some white families</u> took **their** <u>children</u> out of public schools and sent **them** to private schools.
3. Sometimes <u>white customers</u> in the restaurants shouted at <u>the students</u>, threw food at **them**, or hit **them**, but <u>the students</u> continued **their** protests.
4. In one famous incident at an all-white restaurant in North Carolina, <u>black and white students</u> organized a protest called a sit-in. **They** simply sat in the restaurant until the African American customers were served. There were many <u>sit-ins</u>. Sometimes **they** lasted for days.

5. The anger sometimes led to violence against the protesters and even against blacks in general. Protests expanded and the violence against **them** also increased.

3 Answering short-answer test questions Page 122

B

Sample sentences:

a. Analyze the first paragraph of the Declaration of Independence.
b. Describe some of the segregation policies that were common in the American South after the Civil War.
c. Compare perspectives on the definition of equality at the time of the War for Independence and after the Civil War.

D

1. The lawyers defending segregation in the *Brown versus Board of Education of Topeka* case offered two main arguments.
2. The strategies of the civil rights movement included court battles and street protests.
3. The economies of the Northern and Southern states before the U.S. Civil War were very different.

4 Reading boxed texts Page 123

A

1. African Americans
2. *Answers will vary.*
3. a raisin in the sun, a sore, rotten meat, a syrupy sweet, a heavy load
4. *Answers wil vary.*
5. *Answers will vary.*

Chapter 5 Academic Vocabulary Review

Page 124

1. violation
2. issues
3. excluded
4. incidents
5. inherently
6. evident
7. transportation
8. eventually
9. section
10. pursuit

Developing Writing Skills

Pages 125–126

C

Sample answers:

I. Voting rights
II. Use of public facilities
III. Education

E

Sample answers:

I. Voting Rights
   A. After Civil War – many barriers to voting, for ex. poll taxes, literacy tests, and grandfather laws
   B. 1960s and later – courts ruled that these were all illegal; greater equality in voting
II. Use of public facilities
   A. 1870–1960s – segregated, facilities for blacks much worse than facilities for whites
   B. 1960s and later – Supreme Court ruled segregation of public facilities in violation of Fourteenth Amendment
III. Education
   A. 1870–1960s – segregated, schools for blacks much worse than facilities for whites
   B. 1960s and later – Bd vs. Topeka B of Ed ended legal segregation

F

Sample paragraph:

After the Civil War and until the middle of the twentieth century, many African Americans were forced to use separate and inferior public facilities. One of the major battles of the civil rights movement was to end this practice. Before the civil rights movement, African Americans had to sit in separate areas in buses and trains and use separate bathrooms and drinking fountains. Many businesses, such as restaurants and hotels, would not serve African Americans. The civil rights movement protested against this unfair treatment. There were protest marches and sit-ins to bring attention to unfair treatment of African Americans. The court system was used to fight against it. These strategies helped lead to changes in federal and state laws as well as in the attitudes of many Americans.

Chapter 6
The Struggle Continues

Reading 1 – What Does Equality Mean Today?

Preparing to Read

Understanding key terms Page 127
A and B

1. d   2. e   3. b   4. c   5. a

After You Read

1 Reading for main ideas Page 131
A

2, 5

2 Understanding text structure Page 131
A

1. Par. 2   2. Par. 4   3. Par. 5   4. Par. 3
5. Par. 1

B

University of California: reject; Allan Bakke: argue;
Abigail Fisher: argue

3 Synonyms Page 132
A

1. …the government should ensure that there are not only equal opportunities and resources for minorities but also equal results . . .

2. …everyone should have an equal chance to succeed and to compete for resources.

3. A third perspective on equality is that there should be equal outcomes.

4. Perhaps the African American children are more likely to be from poor families who cannot give them the support they need to succeed in school.

5. The second view . . . says that we are all different, but none of these differences matters . . .

B

1. guarantee   4. provide
2. opportunity   5. perspective
3. results

4 Markers of relationship Page 133
A

1. regardless of   3. despite/in spite of
2. depending on   4. based on

B

Sample answers:

1. His decision was based on his past experience with the company.

2. Regardless of your opinion, you should listen to what other people have to say.

3. Depending on the weather, we may be able to eat lunch outside.

4. He decided to take the job in spite of the low salary.

Reading 2 – Equal Rights and Protection for All

After You Read

1 Reading for details Page 138
A

Sample answers:
Progress details are underlined once; challenge details are underlined twice.

Women

Women were the first to use the strategies that had been successful in the civil rights movement: protests, boycotts, and political pressure. As a result, since the 1960s, women have achieved some degree of equality. For example, before the women's movement began, far more men than women attended college. Today, significantly more women than men attend college; the number of men and women attending law, medical, and business schools is almost equal. Women today make up about half of the labor force, and some have become leaders in government and business. By law, employers may no longer discriminate based on gender; in fact, they may not specify gender or age in job advertisements. (Par. 2)

Nevertheless, <u>there is still a gap between men and women, particularly in the workplace</u>. The estimates of the gap vary. For men and women working in the same profession, the gap is smaller. However, according to the U.S. Bureau of Labor Statistics, when comparing all men and women regardless of occupation, women who work full-time <u>earn just 77 cents for every dollar that men with equal experience earn for equal work</u>. For example, on average, if a man earns $100,000 to do a job, a woman receives just $77,000 for the same job. This results in a lifetime difference of $431,000 in wages. Although women make up half of the labor force, <u>80 percent of them work in job categories that have the lowest pay</u>. There have been many improvements in the status of women, but inequalities remain. Perhaps the most important achievement of the women's movement is that <u>girls who are born today expect an equal chance for success</u>. (Par. 3)

Disabled

Therefore, it has not always been easy for the disabled to gain access to education and employment. There is a <u>strong relationship between disability and low income, low levels of education, and unemployment</u>. Over the past 40 years, people with disabilities have fought for equal protection and treatment. Their battle has been difficult but has had positive results. Today, <u>federal and many state laws prohibit companies, governments, and institutions from discriminating against people with disabilities</u>. (Par. 4)

The 1990 Americans with Disabilities Act (ADA) protects people with disabilities against discrimination in several areas. In employment, it states that if a person with a disability is qualified to do a particular job, <u>the employer must accommodate that person, that is, the employer must offer reasonable assistance for that worker</u>. For example, a worker in a wheelchair might need a special desk. This kind of accommodation can be expensive, and many employers have resisted these changes in spite of the law. (Par. 5)

<u>The ADA also states that public places and transportation must provide access for people with disabilities so that they can participate in daily life</u>. (Par. 6)

Older adults

Federal law also prohibits discrimination against people because of their age, specifically, against people who are 40 years old or older. <u>This means that employers cannot base decisions about hiring, pay, or promotion on an employee's age</u>. Similarly, a worker cannot be fired <u>because he or she is "too old."</u> <u>Advertisements for jobs cannot specify age as a requirement</u>. This does not mean that ageism – discrimination based on age – does not exist. When the economy is weak, employers often

reduce their workforce. They may fire older workers, who often cost employers more than younger workers, without providing a reason. Older workers who lose their jobs, particularly those over 50, generally have more difficulty finding a new job than younger workers. <u>Experts say that age discrimination remains more acceptable in the workplace than discrimination based on race or gender</u>. When employers say they want "fresh ideas" in their business, they often mean they want younger, cheaper workers. (Par. 7)

2 Writing about examples Page 139

A

- In other words, these laws state that it is illegal to discriminate against people based on specific characteristics, <u>such as</u> race, religion, national origin, gender, age, and disability. (Par. 1)
- <u>For example</u>, before the women's movement began, far more men than women attended college. (Par. 2)
- <u>For example</u>, on average, if a man earns $100,000 to do a job, a woman receives just $77,000 for the same job. (Par. 3)
- It is estimated that more than 50 million Americans – 19 percent of the population – have some form of physical or mental disability, <u>such as</u> blindness or depression. (Par. 4)
- <u>For example</u>, a worker in a wheelchair might need a special desk. (Par. 5)
- <u>For example</u>, buildings must provide accommodations <u>such as</u> accessible bathrooms and ramps for people in wheelchairs. (Par. 6)

B

1. X   2. √   3. X   4. √   5. X   6. √

3 Prepositions with verbs Page 140

A

1. on	5. against
2. against	6. for
3. in	7. for
4. to	8. in

B

Sample answers:

1. African Americans have struggled for equal treatment.
2. The Supreme Court decision resulted in changes in state laws.
3. Federal law prohibits employers from making decisions based on race.

4 Writing about obligations and recommendations Pages 140–141

A

Reading 2

■ . . . if a person with a disability is qualified to do a particular job, the employer must accommodate that person; that is, the employer must offer reasonable assistance for that worker.

■ . . . public places and transportation must provide access for people with disabilities so that they can participate in daily life.

■ For example, buildings must provide accommodations . . . . Buses and trains must also provide access to the disabled.

Reading 1

■ . . . Americans should all have an equal opportunity to compete for resources such as jobs, housing, and education.

■ Resources . . . should be distributed to ensure all Americans achieve the same level of success.

■ . . . everyone should have an equal chance to succeed and to compete for resources.

■ A third perspective on equality is that there should be equal outcomes.

■ . . . the government should ensure that there are not only equal opportunities and resources for minorities but also equal results, that is, that the outcomes should be a more equal share in life . . .

■ Should the city simply guarantee a certain number of positions in the police department to women?

■ On the other hand, they believe that hard work and merit – not membership in a specific group – should be the reason one person does well and another person does not.

C

Sample answers:

1. Employers should make sure that all the employees have a chance to succeed.

2. Schools should offer all children a good education.

D

Sample answers:

1. Employers must not consider race when they hire new workers.

2. The government must provide equal services to everyone.

5 Applying what you have read Page 141

3, 6

Reading 3 – How Equal Are We Now?

Preparing to Read

2 Examining graphics Page 142

A

1. household income
2. Latino, African American, White

B

1. White
2. African American
3. *Answers will vary.*
4. *Answers will vary.*

After You Read

1 Reading about statistics Page 146

A

	Percent that ...	1970	1980	2010
African Americans	graduated from college		8	19
	lived in poverty			36
	owned a home			45
	had a household income above $150,000			4.0
Latinos	graduated from college	4.5		14
	lived in poverty			35
	owned a home			48
	had a household income above $150,000			4.2
Whites	graduated from college			30
	lived in poverty			14
	owned a home			74
	had a household income above $150,000			12.6

2 Writing about statistics Page 147

B

Sample answers:
- It is estimated that 30 percent of Latinos earn less than $25,000 a year.
- Household income above $150,000 for Latinos in 2010 was estimated to be 4.2%.

3 Synonyms Page 147

A

1. big/bigger
   - (Par.1) large
   - (Par.4) considerable
   - (Par.6) substantial
2. a lot (adv.)
   - (Par.4) substantially
   - (Par.4) considerably
3. is connected to
   - (Par.1) is related to
   - (Par.3) is associated with
   - (Par.3) is linked to

B

Sample answers:
- There was substantial increase in the rise in college graduation rates among African Americans between 1980 and 2010.
- The rate of home ownership is linked to income levels.

Chapter 6 Academic Vocabulary Review

Page 148

1. perspectives
2. visibility
3. distribute
4. media
5. achieve
6. status
7. benefits
8. purchases
9. integrate
10. promotion

Practicing Academic Writing

Now Write

Pages 151–152

A and B

Sample introductions:
Equality is a very complicated issue. Many Americans disagree about its meaning.
Some groups no longer need the extra help to guarantee their success. With access to educational and job opportunities, most groups can succeed. However, some groups do need extra assistance to make sure that there is an equal playing field.

Sample paragraphs:
  In the past, there was a lot of discrimination against different ethnic groups, so it was hard for them to be successful. Because of this past discrimination, there were special programs to make it easier for them to get a good education or a good job. Today, everyone has an equal chance of success so we don't need these programs anymore for most protected groups.
  Success in work and life should be due to merit. Special programs that make it easier for ethnic groups to get a good education or a good job are unfair to the groups who don't get the special treatment. Disabled people are a different category, however. They have special challenges that make it difficult for them to compete with people who are not disabled. Therefore, the government must ensure that businesses and schools give them extra help so they have an equal chance for a good life.

Chapter 7
A History of American Values

Reading 1 – The Roots of American Values

Preparing to Read

1 Increasing reading speed Page 156
D

1. a, d, e, f, g, h
2. a. F   b. T   c. T   d. F

After You Read

2 Understanding key terms Page 160
A

1. d	3. a	5. f	7. b
2. e	4. g	6. h	8. c

B

1. self-reliance
2. egalitarianism
3. risks
4. optimism
5. ambition
6. self-discipline
7. individualism
8. Values

3 Noun + infinitive phrases Pages 161–162
A

1. all people should have (an equal chance) to succeed
2. a belief in the power of (individuals) to control their own lives
3. you have the (ability) to control your own future
4. in their (desire) to make their own choices

B

1. All people should have (an equal chance) to succeed.
2. The Constitution gives Congress the (power) to create courts.
3. It seemed to be a land of endless opportunity for someone with a good idea and the (willingness) to take a risk.
4. A fundamental value is in (the right of individuals) to make their own decisions.
5. Many settlers believed it was (their destiny) to populate the land from one coast to the other.
6. Native Americans understood (their responsibility) to care for the land.

C

Sample answers:

- Many Americans believe that they have the ability to control their own future.
- In the United States, most people believe that all people should have an equal chance to succeed.

4 Applying what you have read Page 162
B

Sample answers:

1. a
2. c
3. a
4. b
5. b
6. d
7. a, b, c
8. a, b
9. b, d
10. a, b, d

Reading 2 – The American West

Preparing to Read

2 Understanding key terms Page 163
A

1. frontier	3. pioneers	5. wilderness
2. myth	4. destiny	6. cede

After You Read

1 Reading for details Page 167
B

Sample answers:

Evidence for each value is underlined once.

- self-reliance

Only the toughest and most self-reliant pioneers did well in these circumstances. They had to be able to build houses for themselves, farm, raise animals, hunt for food, and protect themselves and their property. (Par. 3)

- taking risks

However, this search for a new life had a cost. The westward journey and life in the West were dangerous and difficult . . . About 40,000 people died along the western trails from illness, hunger, and cold. One of them, the Oregon Trail, has been called the nation's longest graveyard. (Par. 3)

- optimism

For these people, the West, which meant land west of the Mississippi River, seemed to be a place of unlimited opportunity and resources: excellent farmland and land rich in minerals, thick forests, and plenty of animals for hunting. The land and the sky seemed to stretch without end, waiting for them. . . They dreamed of being free of civilization and of living in open places. (Par. 2)

- egalitarianism

A final important characteristic of the frontier was its social equality. In the struggle to survive, success depended on the pioneers' individual strength and resourcefulness, not on money or family background. (Par. 3)

2 Examining graphics   Page 167
B

1. a. 2   b. 3   c. 1   d. 4
2. treaty and annexation
3. b

3 *Few* and *a few*   Page 168
A

- Few images have as powerful a place in the American imagination as the symbols of the American West, such as the covered wagon, the log cabin, and the cowboy. (Par. 1)
- There were many physical hardships and few comforts or conveniences on the western trails. (Par. 3)

B

not many/not enough

Sample clues:

have as powerful; many physical hardships

C

1. not many – clue = *disappointed*, a negative
2. some – clue = *excited*, a positive

D

1. few   2. a few   3. a few   4. few

4 Word families   Page 169
A

Sample answers:

1. rely   2. resource   3. population
4. expand   5. cede

Reading 3 – The Business of Success

After You Read

1 Answering multiple-choice questions   Page 174

1. a, b   2. d   3. b   4. d

2 Writing about change   Page 175
A

Verb of direction	What went up or down?	Who/what controlled it?
reduced (line 22)	competition	Carnegie
decrease (line 36)	competition	Rockefeller
reduce (line 42)	power of monopolies	federal government
increased (line 66)	competition for remaining jobs	new technology
declined (line 67)	wages	new technology
increased (line 69)	competition for jobs	large number of immigrants
expand (line 83)	power	the struggle
raise (line 90)	pay levels	union victories
expand (line 91)	benefits	union victories

3 Collocations   Page 176
A

1. take   2. achieve   3. make, invest, save
4. face   5. lose   6. win

B

1. face   2. achieve   3. win/lose
4. take   5. achieve   6. face

4 Understanding cartoons Page 176

A

Sample answers:

1. Standard Oil's reach and influence are best shown by the tentacles of the octopus.

2. The White House and the Capitol (government buildings) – Standard Oil controlled the government, not the other way around.

3. It has too much power.

Chapter 7 Academic Vocabulary Review

Page 177

1. injuries
2. invested
3. acquired
4. attitude
5. images

6. alternatives
7. consistent
8. implication
9. preceded
10. persisted

Developing Writing Skills

Page 179

F

1. The spirit of invention and innovation has been an important theme throughout American history.

2. Innovation in medicine. Innovation in industry.

Chapter 8
American Values Today

Reading 1 – The Individual and Society: Rights and Responsibilities

After You Read

1 Reading for main ideas Page 184
A

2

B

1. individual rights versus the good of society
2. self-reliance versus government support and assistance

C

1. individual rights versus the good of society

(a) eminent domain; (b) national security concerns

2. self-reliance versus government support and assistance

(a) New Deal; (b) ARRA

2 Applying what you have read Page 184
B

1. a   2. c   3. b

3 Understanding text structure Page 185

1. 2   2. 3–6   3. 1   4. 7

4 Prepositions Page 185
A

1. from/against
2. with
3. to
4. on
5. to
6. on
7. for/on
8. on

5 Collocations Pages 185–186
A

1. accept/have
2. provide/increase
3. get
4. gather
5. take
6. perform
7. play
8. pay

B

1. collects
2. take
3. collect
4. give
5. need

6 Responding to a quote Page 186
C

Sample answer:

The quote is related to the second issue in the text: self-reliance versus government assistance. It shows President Johnson's understanding that one important role of the government is to provide assistance to those who need it. Not everyone can be self-reliant all of the time.

Reading 2 – The Open Road and Car Culture

Preparing to Read

2 Scanning Page 187
A

1. fewer than 5 million
2. 77%
3. 90%
4. 42,000 miles
5. SUVs
6. 3 trillion

After You Read

1 Answering true/false questions Page 190
A and B

1. F (1)   3. T (3)   5. T (4)   7. T (2)
2. T (2)   4. T (3)   6. F (4)   8. F (5)

2 Reading for details Page 190
A

3 The government built good roads so people could get from their homes to their jobs in the city.
4 More people moved to the suburbs because there were lots of good roads.

1 People moved to the suburbs where there were good, inexpensive houses.
2 People who lived in the suburbs needed cars because there was little public transportation.

3 Writing about reasons Page 191

A

- First, the price of cars dropped significantly (because of) new technology and new methods for manufacturing cars (Par. 2)
- Most people needed to drive (because) there was little public transportation from the suburbs to their jobs in the city. (Par. 3)
- More recently, the popularity of SUVs has declined, partly (because) they use a lot of gasoline. (Par. 4)

B

Sample answers:

1. their religious beliefs
2. because
3. because of
4. they didn't want to send their children to school with African American children.
5. their image
6. because

4 Gerunds Page 192

A

1. Americans feel that driving a car means the freedom to come and go wherever they choose. S
2. First, the price of cars dropped significantly because of new technology and new methods for manufacturing cars. P
3. Owning a car became essential for daily life. S
4. Many people want to show they are concerned about the environment and saving energy. P

B

Sample answers:

1. learning
2. Owning
3. building
4. Assisting
5. driving

Reading 3 – Is the American Dream Still Possible?

After You Read

1 Reading actively Page 198

B

Sample answers:

Cue	Questions for active readers	Action
Education and **upward mobility** (Title)	This is the title so it must be the topic. What is the relationship between them?	*Look for evidence of this relationship: terms such as college, higher, success, increase, improve*
In the recent **past** . . . (line 2)	Does this mean I will also learn about the present?	*Look for signals like today or now.*
however . . . (line 3)	What is the contrast to this history?	*Look for a contrasting statement that there may no longer be jobs for people with no college education*
Most jobs with higher pay in the twenty-first century **require at least some higher education.** (line 5)	Why is this important? What are the implications of this statement?	*Look for evidence of changes in trends in higher education.*

2 Word families Page 199

1. secure
2. Poverty
3. mobile
4. certainty
5. ability
6. equal

3 Writing definitions Page 200

B

Sample answers:

1. A *meritocracy* is a system that rewards effort and talent.
2. A *property tax* is a tax that is based on the value of property.
3. A *consumer nation* is a country that consumes more than it produces.

C

Sample answers:

2.

a. *Upward* economic and social *mobility* means improving your financial and social situation.
b. *Optimism* means feeling positive about the future.
c. *Self-discipline* means making yourself do important things even when you don't want to.
d. *Vertical integration* means controlling all aspects of an industry to decrease competition.

Chapter 8 Academic Vocabulary Review

Page 201

1. proportional
2. recovered
3. vehicles
4. previous
5. consumers
6. financial
7. style
8. available
9. survey
10. trend

Practicing Academic Writing

Now Write

Pages 203–204

Sample paragraphs:

Every culture has a set of beliefs that guides behavior and attitudes. The "American Dream" reflects many of these beliefs in the United States. The "American Dream" is a set of many ideas, but the most important are the belief in the basic equality of all people and the belief in the importance of working hard to get what you want.

Probably the most fundamental belief in American culture is in equality. This belief first appeared in writing in the Constitution, and Abraham Lincoln repeated it 100 years later in the Gettysburg Address. This belief that everyone starts in the same place remains important today in both the attitudes of the public and government policies.

Like the belief in basic equality, the value of hard work is a central theme in American culture, especially in economic success. Leaders in business who have worked hard have often been very successful. Sometimes they have started with very little money. They just had a good idea and they were willing to work hard. We can see examples of this in the past, for example, Andrew Carnegie and John Rockefeller, and in technology companies today such as Microsoft and Google.

Americans' egalitarian values and their work ethic are central to the belief that their future and their success is in their own hands.

Name: _____

Date: _____

Unit 1 • Content Quiz

Part 1 True/False questions (24 points)

Decide if the following statements are true (T) or false (F).

_____ 1. The President of the United States writes the country's laws.

_____ 2. The United States government is prohibited from supporting any particular religion.

_____ 3. The President of the United States cannot run for re-election.

_____ 4. There are more than 70 million guns in American homes.

_____ 5. After the War of Independence, Americans wanted a strong central government.

_____ 6. The Supreme Court is part of the judicial branch of government.

Part 2 Multiple choice questions (24 points)

Circle the best answer from the choices listed.

1. Which of the following factors does *not* explain why the first settlers came to the American colonies?

   a. for religious freedom

   b. to escape from war

   c. for greater social equality

   d. for economic opportunity

2. The First Amendment to the Constitution guarantees

   a. the privacy of all citizens.

   b. protection for people accused of crimes.

   c. the right to own a gun.

   d. freedom of religion.

3. Only the federal government, and not state governments,

   a. controls the military.

   b. collects taxes.

   c. makes laws for business.

   d. pays for schools.

4. In colonial America, militias were originally formed to

   a. hunt wild animals and provide food.

   b. protect the settlers.

   c. fight wars.

   d. support the Constitution.

Part 3 Short answer questions (24 points)

Write a short answer to each of the following questions. In most cases no more than one or two sentences are required.

1. What is a *federalist* system of government?

2. What is *hate speech*?

3. What is the purpose of the Bill of Rights?

Part 4 One paragraph answer (28 points)

Choose one of the following topics and write a paragraph about it. Use a separate sheet of paper.

1. The system of checks and balances as a fundamental part of the American government

2. The limits on freedom of speech in the United States

Unit 2 • Content Quiz

Part 1 True/False questions (24 points)

Decide if the following statements are true (T) or false (F).

_____ 1. The average life of a slave was half as long as the average life of a white person.

_____ 2. Today the largest number of legal immigrants comes from Mexico and China.

_____ 3. Immigrants who arrived in the United States in the last half of the nineteenth century found good jobs that paid well.

_____ 4. Whites are now a minority in the United States.

_____ 5. Native Americans have lost most of the land they once owned.

_____ 6. Most unauthorized immigrants in the United States come from Mexico.

Part 2 Multiple choice questions (24 points)

Circle the best answer from the choices listed.

1. *Triangular trade* involved

    a. Africa, Portugal, and the American colonies.

    b. Africa, South America, and North America.

    c. Africa, the Caribbean, and cities in North America.

    d. the Caribbean, New York, and London.

2. In the eighteenth century, the largest number of immigrants to the United States came from

    a. southern and eastern Europe.

    b. China and Japan.

    c. Canada and Mexico.

    d. western Europe.

3. A great percentage increase of Latinos in the United States between 2000 and 2010 occurred

    a. in the Southeast.

    b. on both coasts.

    c. in California.

    d. Mexico, Arizona, and Texas.

4. One important part of the government's policy of assimilation of Native Americans was

    a. a series of treaties with native tribes.

    b. the removal of 4,000 Cherokee to Oklahoma.

    c. the establishment of reservations.

    d. boarding schools where native children learned white culture.

Part 3 Short answer questions (24 points)

Write a short answer to each of the following questions. In most cases no more than one or two sentences are required.

1. Describe the differences between the Asian American population of today and the Asian population of one hundred years ago.

2. What are two arguments against the continued high rate of immigration to the United States?

3. Name three groups of people who profited from slavery.

Part 4 One paragraph answer (28 points)

Choose one of the following topics and write a paragraph about it. Use a separate sheet of paper.

1. The ethnic and racial diversity of the United States in 2050

2. Reasons for the continued illegal immigration to the United States

Unit 3 • Content Quiz

Part 1 True/False questions (24 points)

Decide if the following statements are true (T) or false (F).

_____ 1. Jim Crow laws prevented many Southern blacks from voting.

_____ 2. Discrimination against African Americans ended when the Civil
Rights Act of 1964 became law.

_____ 3. Many people with disabilities have low education and low income
levels.

_____ 4. The percentages of African Americans, Latinos, and whites who are
poor is about the same.

_____ 5. After *Brown versus Board of Education of Topeka*, black and white
children all went to the same schools in the South.

_____ 6. Women and African Americans were not included in statements about
equality in the Declaration of Independence and the Constitution.

Part 2 Multiple choice questions (24 points)

Circle the best answer from the choices listed.

1. *Brown versus Board of Education of Topeka* was a court case that

    a. gave equal voting rights to African Americans.

    b. integrated buses and trains in the American South.

    c. ended legal segregation in schools.

    d. settled the boycott of buses in Alabama.

2. Which is *not* given as a possible reason for the low graduation rates for
Latinos?

    a. It is difficult to study in a second language.

    b. Schools in Latino neighborhoods are often crowded.

    c. Latino parents cannot help their children in school.

    d. Schools in Latino neighborhoods don't have as many resources.

3. Since the 1960s, women have achieved many goals in their fight for equality.
One goal they have *not* achieved is

    a. equal pay for equal work.

    b. equal representation in colleges and universities.

    c. greater representation in government.

    d. greater representation in the workforce.

4. Until the 1960s, discrimination against African Americans was

   a. practiced only in the South.

   b. based on the Thirteenth Amendment.

   c. a result of the Civil War.

   d. accepted throughout the country.

Part 3 Short answer questions (24 points)

Write a short answer to each of the following questions. In most cases no more than one or two sentences are required.

1. Name two ways to measure progress toward equality of different groups in the United States.

2. Name three barriers that prevented African Americans from voting after amendments to the Constitution gave them the right to vote.

3. Name three ways that society can accommodate the disabled.

Part 4 One paragraph answer (28 points)

Choose one of the following topics and write a paragraph about it. Use a separate sheet of paper.

1. The different ways in which equality can be understood

2. The direction the United States is going in—is it becoming more or less equal?

Unit 4 • Content Quiz

Part 1 True/False questions (24 points)

Decide if the following statements are true (T) or false (F).

_____ 1. New technology in the nineteenth century helped factory workers by increasing wages.

_____ 2. The founders of the United States believed that people should be judged by what they do, not by where they come from.

_____ 3. Ninety percent of Americans own a car.

_____ 4. The federal government can take away private property if the property will be used for a public purpose.

_____ 5. Most Americans believe that hard work and ambition are the most important factors in success.

_____ 6. In the eighteenth century, the belief in the importance of the individual was widespread.

Part 2 Multiple choice questions (24 points)

Circle the best answer from the choices listed.

1. Factory owners opposed trade unions because

    a. trade unions increased competition.

    b. trade unions tried to get better pay and better conditions for workers.

    c. trade unions opposed new technology.

    d. trade unions fought against monopolies.

2. What kind of tax is controlled by local communities—cities and towns?

    a. sales tax

    b. income tax

    c. property tax

    d. business tax

3. During the Great Depression, the New Deal

    a. provided jobs for the unemployed.

    b. increased taxes for the rich.

    c. provided health care for the poor.

    d. increased educational opportunities for all children.

Photocopiable

4. During the westward expansion,

    a. many people became rich.

    b. many pioneers died.

    c. three million people moved west of the Mississippi.

    d. many Native Americans started farms.

Part 3 Short answer questions (24 points)

Write a short answer to each of the following questions. In most cases no more than one or two sentences are required.

1. Give two reasons why settlers moved west.

2. Describe three problems that factory workers faced in the nineteenth century.

3. What is the role of taxes in education in the United States today?

Part 4 One paragraph answer (28 points)

Choose one of the following topics and write about it. Use a separate sheet of paper.

1. How Carnegie and Rockefeller achieved their great success

2. The conflict between individual rights and what is best for society

Content Quiz Answer Keys

Unit 1

Part 1 True/False questions (24 points)

1. F   2. T   3. F
4. T   5. F   6. T

Part 2 Multiple choice questions (24 points)

1. b   2. d
3. a   4. b

Part 3 Short answer questions (24 points)

1. A federalist system of government divides power and responsibility between the central and state governments.

2. Hate speech is hurtful or negative statements directed against a group because of a specific characteristic of that group such as race or religion.

3. The purpose of the Bill of Rights is to protect the rights of individuals, especially from any abuse of power by the government.

Part 4 One paragraph answer (28 points)

1. The response should discuss the three branches of government, their powers, and the checks by which each branch limits the powers of the others.

2. The response should include the idea that one person's freedom of speech ends when it causes clear harm to another person. It should include examples of dangerous and libelous speech.

Unit 2

Part 1 True/False questions (24 points)

1. T   2. T   3. F
4. F   5. T   6. T

Part 2 Multiple choice questions (24 points)

1. c   2. d
3. a   4. d

Part 3 Short answer questions (24 points)

1. Answers should include the idea that in the past Asians came to escape economic conditions in their countries, they took jobs here with low pay, and they did not have much education.

2. Answers should include two of the following arguments: drain on government resources, competition for jobs, and dilution of national identity including language use.

3. Answers should include three of the following groups: slave traders, ship owners, rum producers, cotton farmers, clothing factory owners, and people who bought cotton clothing.

Part 4 One paragraph answer (28 points)

1. Answers should include the idea that as a larger number of immigrants come from Latin America and Asia, they will continue to take a larger percentage of the overall population. The white population (non-Latino) will likely not be the majority group in the U.S. at that time.

2. The response should include the notion that as long as there are dramatic economic differences between the United States and the developing world, immigration, both authorized and unauthorized, will continue. Immigrants will come for better economic opportunities, and the United States will need the cheap labor that they provide.

Unit 3

Part 1 True/False questions (24 points)

1. T   2. F   3. T
4. F   5. F   6. T

Part 2 Multiple choice questions (24 points)

1. c   2. c
3. a   4. d

Part 3 Short answer questions (24 points)

1. Answers should refer to two of the following: educational attainment, economic profiles, and representation in government.

2. Answers should refer to literacy tests, voting taxes, and grandfather laws.

3. Answers can include any of the following: The government can provide assistance in education, transportation, and communication. Businesses can assist by hiring the disabled and providing special equipment necessary for them to do their jobs. Government, business, and public institutions can accommodate the disabled by providing easy access, for example, ramps, elevators, and special parking places.

Part 4 One paragraph answer (28 points)

1. The response should include the three interpretations discussed in the text: (1) all people are essentially the same, and therefore, equal; (2) everyone should have equal opportunity and access; and (3) there should be a guarantee of equal outcomes.

2. This response is the most subjective of all of the quiz items so far and will allow the most latitude, but it should include support for the position taken. A "more egalitarian" response should refer to the recent progress in education and economic status by minorities. A "less egalitarian" response should refer to the remaining gap between majority and minority and between rich and poor. The response might include some discussion of the institutional structures that suggest the groups will remain apart with regard to, for example, school funding.

Unit 4

Part 1 True/False questions (24 points)

1. F   2. T   3. T
4. T   5. T   6. F

Part 2 Multiple choice questions (24 points)

1. b   2. c
3. a   4. b

Part 3 Short answer questions (24 points)

1. The response should include two of the following: Many settlers moved west to find good farmland and to get away from big cities. Many thought of the West as a land of unlimited economic opportunities and resources, such as minerals, forests, and animals. Students may also mention the dream of a freer life than life in the cities had become, and the search for a place in which social class was even less important.

2. Responses should include three of the following: wages were low, there were no benefits, factories were dangerous, and there was a lot of competition for jobs.

3. The response should state that education is funded by taxes on property. It should also include the idea that poorer communities have lower property values; they generate lower tax revenues so there are fewer resources for education in these communities.

Part 4 One paragraph answer (28 points)

1. The response should include the concepts of vertical integration and monopoly. It might include mention of hard work and ambition. Students might also infer something about opposition to unions, which is implicit, but not explicitly stated in the reading.

2. The response should refer to the fact that laws and policies that protect and provide for individuals may go against the interests of society as a whole. The response should include historical and current examples of this conflict, for example, eminent domain and national security.